MAXIMS AND HINTS

FOR

AN ANGLER;

AND

MISERIES OF FISHING.

TO WHICH ARE ADDED

MAXIMS AND HINTS FOR A CHESS PLAYER,

BY

RICHARD PENN, Esq., F.R.S.

With Wood-Cuts.

A NEW EDITION, ENLARGED.

LONDON :

JOHN MURRAY, ALBEMARLE STREET.

MDCCCXXXIX.

BEGINNING EARLY.

THE FOLLOWING EXTRACTS

FROM THE

Common-Place-Book

OF THE

HOUGHTON FISHING CLUB

ARE RESPECTFULLY DEDICATED

TO HIS

BROTHER ANGLERS

BY A

MEMBER OF THE CLUB.

LONDON,
March, 1833.

MAXIMS AND HINTS

FOR

AN ANGLER.

B

" You see the ways the fisherman doth take
" To catch the fish ; what engines doth he make ?
" Behold ! how he engageth all his wits,
" Also his snares, lines, angles, hooks, and nets :
" Yet fish there be, that neither hook nor line,
" Nor snare, nor net, nor engine can make thine ;
" They must be groped for, and be tickled too,
" Or they will not be catch'd, whate`er you do."

JOHN BUNYAN

" And when he shows them to you, do not show yourself to them."

To face page 3.

MAXIMS AND HINTS

FOR

AN ANGLER:

BY

A BUNGLER.

[Loosely thrown out, in order to provoke contradiction,
and elicit truth from the expert.]

I.

ARE there any fish in the river to which you
are going?

II.

Having settled the above question in the
affirmative, get some person who knows the
water to show you whereabout the fish usually
lie; and when he shows them to you, do not
show yourself to them.

B 2

III.

Comparatively coarse fishing will succeed better when you are not seen by the fish, than the finest when they see you.

IV.

Do not imagine that, because a fish does not instantly dart off on first seeing you, he is the less aware of your presence; he almost always on such occasions ceases to feed, and pays you the compliment of devoting his whole attention to you, whilst he is preparing for a start whenever the apprehended danger becomes sufficiently imminent.

V.

By wading when the sun does not shine, you may walk in the river within eighteen or twenty yards below a fish, which would be immediately driven away by your walking on the bank on either side, though at a greater distance from him.

VI.

When you are fishing with the natural May-fly, it is as well to wait for a passing cloud, as to drive away the fish by putting your fly to him in the glare of the sunshine, when he will not take it.

VII.

If you pass your fly neatly and well three times over a trout, and he refuses it, do not wait any longer for him : you may be sure that he has seen the line of invitation which you have sent over the water to him, and does not intend to come.

VIII.

If your line be nearly *taut,* as it ought to be, with little or no gut in the water, a good fish will always hook himself, on your gently raising the top of the rod when he has taken the fly.

IX.

If you are above a fish in the stream when you hook him, get below him as soon as you can ; and remember that if you pull him, but for an instant, against the stream, he will, if a heavy fish, break his hold ; or if he should be firmly hooked, you will probably find that the united strength of the stream and fish is too much for your skill and tackle.

X.

I do not think that a fish has much power of stopping himself if, immediately on being hooked, he is moved slowly with the current, under the attractive influence of your rod and line. He will soon find that a forced march of this sort is very fatiguing, and he may then be brought, by a well-regulated exercise of gentle violence, to the bank, from whence he is to be instantly whipt out by an expert assistant, furnished with a landing-net, the ring of which ought not to be of a

"Whence he is to be instantly whipt out by an expert assistant, furnished," &c.

To face page 8

less diameter than eighteen inches, the handle of it being seven feet long.

XI.

If, after hooking a trout, you allow him to remain stationary but for a moment, he will have time to put his helm hard a-port or a-starboard, and to offer some resistance. Strong tackle now becomes useful.

XII.

Bear always in mind that no tackle is strong enough, unless well handled. A good fisherman will easily kill a trout of three pounds with a rod and a line which are not strong enough to lift a dead weight of one pound from the floor, and place it on the table.

XIII.

Remember that, in whipping with the artificial fly, it must have time, when you have drawn it out of the water, to make the

whole circuit, and to be at one time straight
behind you, before it can be driven out
straight before you. If you give it the forward impulse too soon, you will hear a crack.
Take this as a hint that your fly is gone to
grass.

XIV.

Never throw with a long line when a short
one will answer your purpose. The most
difficult fish to hook is one which is rising at
three-fourths of the utmost distance to which
you can throw. Even when you are at the
extent of your distance, you have a better
chance; because in this case, when you do
reach him, your line will be straight, and,
when you do not, the intermediate failures
will not alarm him.

XV.

It appears to me that, in whipping with an
artificial fly, there are only two cases in which
a fish taking the fly will infallibly hook himself without your assistance, viz.

1. When your fly first touches the water at the end of a straight line.

2. When you are drawing out your fly for a new throw.

In all other cases it is necessary that, in order to hook him when he has taken the fly, you should do something with your wrist which it is not easy to describe.

XVI.

If your line should fall loose and wavy into the water, it will either frighten away the fish, or he will take the fly into his mouth without fastening himself; and when he finds that it does not answer his purpose, he will spit it out again, before it has answered yours.

XVII.

Although the question of fishing up or down the stream is usually settled by the direction of the wind, you may sometimes

have the option; and it is, therefore, as well
to say a word or two on both sides.

1. If, when you are fishing down-stream,
you take a step or two with each successive
hrow, your fly is always travelling over new
water, which cannot have been disturbed by
the passing of your line.

2. When you are fishing up-stream, you
may lose the advantage of raising so many
fish; but, on the other hand, you will have
a better chance of hooking those which rise
at your fly, because the darting forward of a
fish seizing it has a tendency to tighten your
line, and produce the desired effect.

3. If you are in the habit of sometimes
catching a fish, there is another great advantage in fishing up-stream, viz. whilst you
are playing and leading (necessarily down-
stream) the fish which you have hooked, you

do not alarm the others which are above you, waiting till their turn comes.

XVIII.

The learned are much divided in opinion as to the propriety of whipping with two flies or with one. I am humbly of opinion that your chance of hooking fish is much increased by your using two flies; but I think that, by using only one, you increase your chance of landing the fish.

XIX.

When you are using two flies, you can easily find the bob-fly on the top of the water, and thus be sure that the end-fly is not far off. When you are using only one fly, you cannot so easily see where the fly is ; but I think that you can make a better guess as to where the fish is likely to be after you have hooked him.

XX.

Also, when you are using two flies, you may sometimes catch a fish with one of them, and a weed growing in the river with the other. When such a *liaison* is once formed, you will find it difficult, with all your attractions, to overcome the strong attachment of the fish to your worthless rival the weed.

XXI.

If the weed will not give way in the awkward juncture above alluded to, you must proceed to extremities. " Then comes the tug of war ;" and your line is quite as likely to break between you and the fish, as between the fish and the weed.

XXII.

When, during the season of the May-fly, your friends, the gentlemen from London, say that they " have scarcely seen a fish rise all day," do not too hastily conclude that the fish have not been feeding on the fly.

"You will find it difficult, with all your attractions, to overcome the strong attachment," &c.

To face page 12.

XXIII.

The only " rising" which is seen by the unlearned is the splash which is made by a fish when he darts from a considerable depth in the water to catch an occasional fly on the surface. There is, however, another sort of " rising," which is better worth the skilful angler's attention, viz.

XXIV.

When a fish is seriously feeding on the fly, he stations himself at no greater depth than his own length, and, making his tail the hinge of his motions, he gently raises his mouth to the top of the water, and quietly sucks in the fly attempting to pass over him. A rising of this sort is not easily seen, but it is worth looking for; because, although a fish feeding in this manner will rarely go many inches on either side for a fly, he will as rarely refuse to take one which comes (without any gut in the water) directly to him.

XXV.

If your fly (gut unfortunately included) should swim over a fish without his taking it, look out well for a darting line of undulation, which betokens his immediate departure; and remember, that it is of no use to continue fishing for him after he is gone.

XXVI.

The stations chosen by fish for feeding are those which are likely to afford them good sport in catching flies, viz.

1. The mouths of ditches running into the river.

2. The confluence of two branches of a stream, which has been divided by a patch of weeds.

3. That part of a stream which has been narrowed by two such patches.

4. Fish are also to be found under the bank opposite to the wind, where they are waiting for the flies which are blown against that bank, and fall into the river.

"If a friend should say to you in a careless way, 'Where did you take
that fine fish?'"

To face page 15.

XXVII.

If, during your walks by the river-side, you have marked any good fish, it is fair to presume that other persons have marked them also. Suppose the case of two well-known fish, one of them (which I will call A.) lying above a certain bridge, the other (which I will call B.) lying below the bridge. Suppose further that you have just caught B., and that some curious and cunning friend should say to you in a careless way, " Where did you take that fine fish?" a finished fisherman would advise you to tell your inquiring friend that you had taken your fish just *above* the bridge, describing, as the scene of action, the spot which, in truth, you know to be still occupied by the other fish, A. Your friend would then fish no more for A., supposing that to be the fish which you have caught; and whilst he innocently resumes his operations below the bridge, where he falsely ima-

gines B. still to be, A. is left quietly for you,
if you can catch him.

XXVIII.

When you see a large fish rising so greedily
in the middle of a sharp stream, that you
feel almost sure of his instantly taking your
May-fly, I would advise you to make an ac-
curate survey of all obstructions in the immediate neighbourhood of your feet—of any
ditch which may be close behind you—or of
any narrow plank, amidst high rushes, which
you may shortly have to walk over in a hurry.
If you should hook the fish, a knowledge of
these interesting localities will be very useful
to you.

XXIX.

When your water-proof boots are wet
through, make a hole or two near the bottom
of them, in order that the water, which runs
in whilst you are walking in the river, may
run freely out again whilst you are walking

"A knowledge of these interesting localities will be very useful to you."

To face page 16.

on the bank. You will thus avoid an accompaniment of pumping-music, which is not agreeable.

XXX.

Never mind what they of the old school say about " playing him till he is tired." Much valuable time and many a good fish may be lost by this antiquated proceeding. Put him into your basket *as soon as you can.* Everything depends on the manner in which you commence your acquaintance with him. If you can at first prevail upon him to go a little way down the stream with you, you will have no difficulty afterwards in persuading him to let you have the pleasure of seeing him at dinner.

XXXI.

Do not be afraid of filling your pockets too full when you go out; you are more likely to leave something behind you than to take too much. A man who seldom catches a fish at any other time, usually gets hold of one (and loses him of course) whilst his attendant is gone back for something which had been forgotten.

XXXII

If your attendant is a handy fellow at landing a fish, let him do it in his own way: if he is not, try to find a better man, or go home. Although so much depends upon his skill, you will rarely derive much comfort from asking him for his opinion. If you have had bad sport, and say to him, " Which way shall we go now?" he will most probably say, " Where you please, sir." If you ask him what he thinks of the weather, he is very likely to say that last week (*when you were in London*) it was " famous weather for fishing;" or he will perhaps say, that he expects that next week (*when you are to be at home again*) it will be very good. I never knew one of these men who was satisfied with the present hour.

XXXIII.

Do not leave off fishing early in the evening because your friends are tired. After a bright day, the largest fish are to be caught by whipping between sunset and dark. Even, however, in these precious moments, you will not have good sport if you continue throwing after you have whipped your fly off. Pay attention to this ; and if you have any doubt after dusk, you may easily ascertain the point, by drawing the end of the line quickly through your hand,—particularly if you do not wear gloves.

XXXIV.

No attempt is here made to give directions as to the best seasons for cutting the woods which are fittest for the making of rods, or as to the mode of preparing them ; because the worst rod which is kept for sale at the present day is probably as good as the best of the first few dozen which any amateur is likely to make for himself.

XXXV.

Lastly—When you have got hold of a good fish, which is not very tractable, if you are married, gentle reader, think of your wife, who, like the fish, is united to you by very tender ties, which can only end with her death, or her going into weeds. If you are single, the loss of the fish, when you thought the prize your own, may remind you of some more serious disappointment.

R. P.

Rod Cottage, River Side,
    31st May, 1829.

POSTSCRIPT.

I FORGOT to say, that, if a friend should invite you to his house, saying that he will ·give you " an excellent day's fishing," you ought not to doubt his kind intention, but you certainly ought not to feel very sure that you will have good sport. Provide yourself for such a visit with everything which you may want, as if you were going into an un-inhabited country. Above all things, take a landing-net with you. Your friend's (if he has one) is probably torn and without a handle, being a sort of reticulated shovel for taking fish out of the well of a punt. Take warning from the following story :—

Mr. Jackson and Mr. Thompson went last week to the house of Mr. Jenkins, for a few days' fishing. They were received with the

utmost kindness and hospitality by Mr. and
Mrs. Jenkins, and on the following morning
after breakfast, the gardener (who was on
that day called the fisherman) was desired to
attend them to the river. Thompson, who
had a landing-net of his own, begged to have
a boy to carry it. Jack was immediately
sent for, and he appeared in *top* boots, with
a livery hat and waistcoat.

Arrived at the water-side, Thompson gave
his gnat-basket to the boy, and told him to
go on the other side of the river, and look on
the grass for a few May-flies. Jack said
that he did. not exactly know what May-flies
were, and that the river could not be crossed
without going over a bridge a mile off.
Thompson is a patient man, so he began to
fish with his landing-net for a few May-flies,
and after he had necessarily frightened away
many fish, he succeeded in catching six or
seven May-flies.

Working one of them with the blowing-

The boy exclaiming, " Damn 'un, I miss'd 'un," instantly threw a
second brick-bat.

To face page 23.

line much to his own satisfaction, and think-
ing to extract a compliment from his attendant, he said, " They do not often fish here
in this way—do they ?" " No," said the boy,
" they drags wi' a net ; they did zo the day
afore yesterday."

Our angler, after much patient fishing,
hooked a fine trout; and having brought him
carefully to the bank, he said, " Now, my
lad, don't be in a hurry, but get him out as
soon as you can." Jack ran to the water's
edge, threw down the net, and seizing the
line with both hands, of course broke it immediately.

Nothing daunted, Thompson now mended
his tackle and went on fishing ; and when he
thought, " good easy man," that the very
moment for hooking another trout was arrived, there was a great splash just above his
fly ;—and, the boy exclaiming, " Damn un,
I miss'd un," instantly threw a second brick-
bat at a rat which was crossing the river.

Mine host, in order to accommodate his friends, dined early; and when they went after dinner to enjoy the evening fishing, they found that the miller had turned off the water, and that the river was nearly dry,—so they went back to tea.

R. P.

P. R. Lee, Esq., R A.

MISERIES OF FISHING.

" Quæque ipse miserrima vidi."

MISERIES OF FISHING.

I.

MAKING a great improvement in a receipt which a friend had given you for staining gut—and finding that you have produced exactly the colour which you wanted, but that the dye has made all your bottoms quite rotten.

II.

Suddenly putting up your hand to save your hat in a high wind, and grasping a number of artificial flies, which you had pinned round it, without any intention of taking hold of more than one at a time.

III.

Leading a large fish down-stream and arriving at a ditch, the width of which is evident, although the depth of it may be a

matter of some doubt. Having thus to decide very quickly whether you will lose the
fish and half your tackle, or run the risk of
going up to your neck in mud. Perhaps
both.

IV.

Feeling rather unsteady whilst you are
walking on a windy day over an old foot-
bridge, and having occasion to regret the
decayed state of the hand-rail, which once
protected the passing fisherman.

V.

Fishing for the first time with flies of your
own making—and finding that they are quite
as good as any which you can buy, except
that the hooks are not so firmly tied to the
gut.

VI.

Taking out with you as your aide-de-camp
an unsophisticated lad from the neighbouring
village, who laughs at you when you miss

" And having occasion to regret the decayed state of the hand-rail," &c.

To face page 28.

hooking a fish rising at a fly, and says with a grin, " You can't vasten 'em as my vather does."

VII.

Making the very throw which you feel sure will at last enable you to reach a fish that is rising at some distance—and seeing the upper half of your rod go into the middle of the river.   When you have towed it ashore, finding that it has broken off close to the ferule, which is immoveably fixed in the lower half of your rod.

VIII.

Feeling the first cold drop giving notice to your great toe that in less than two minutes your boot will be full of water.

IX.

Going out on a morning so fine that no man would think of taking his water-proof cloak with him—and then, before catching

any fish, being thoroughly wet through by an
unexpected shower.

X.

When you cannot catch any fish—being
told by your attendant of the excellent sport
which your predecessor had on the same spot,
only a few days before.

XI.

Having brought with you from town a
large assortment of expensive artificial flies—
and being told on showing them to an expe-
rienced native, that " They are certainly very
beautiful, but that none of them are of any
use here."

XII.

After trying in vain to reach a trout which
is rising on the opposite side of the river—
at last walking on; and before you have
gone 100 yards, looking back, and seeing
a more skilful friend catch him at the first
throw.—Weight 3 lbs. 2 oz.

" Looking back, and seeing a more skilful friend catch him at the first throw."

To face page 50

XIII.

Having stupidly trodden on the top of your rod—and then finding that the spare top, which you have brought out with you in the butt, belongs to the rod which you have left at hôme, and will not fit that which you are using.

XIV.

Having steered safely through some very dangerous weeds a fish which you consider to weigh at least 3 lbs., and having brought him safely to the very edge of the bank,—then seeing him, when he is all but in the landing-net, make a plunge, which in a moment renders all your previous skill of no avail, and puts it out of your power to verify the accuracy of your calculations as to his weight.

XV.

Fishing with the blowing-line when the wind is so light that your fly is seldom more than two yards from you, or when the wind is so strong that it always carries your fly up into the air, before it comes to the spot which you wish it to swim over.

XVI.

Wishing to show off before a young friend whom you have been learnedly instructing in the mysteries of the art, and finding that you cannot catch any fish yourself, whilst he (an inexperienced hand) hooks and lands (by mere accident of course) a very large one.

XVII.

Attempting to walk across the river in a new place without knowing exactly whereabouts certain holes, which you have heard of, are. Probing the bottom in front of you with the handle of your landing-net,—and finding it very soft.

"Probing the bottom in front of you with the handle of your landing-net."

To face page 32.

XVIII.

Going some distance for three days' fishing, on the two first of which there is bright sunshine and no wind, and then finding that the third, which opens with " a southerly wind and a cloudy sky," is the day which a neighbouring farmer has fixed upon for washing two hundred sheep on the shallow where you expected to have the best sport.

XIX.

Being allowed to have one day's fishing in a stream, the windings of which are so many, that it would require half a dozen different winds to enable you to fish the greater part of it, from the only side to which your leave extends.

XX.

Finding, on taking your book out of your pocket, that the fly at the end of your line is not the only one by many dozen which you

D

have had in the water, whilst you have been
wading rather too deep.

XXI.

Wading half an inch deeper than the tops
of your boots, and finding afterwards that
you must carry about with you four or five
quarts in each, or must sit down on the wet
grass whilst your attendant pulls them off, in
order that you may empty them, and try to
pull them on again.

XXII.

Jumping out of bed very early every morning, during the season of the May-fly, to look
at a weathercock opposite to your window,
and always finding the wind either in the
north or east.

XXIII.

Having just hooked a heavy fish, when you
are using the blowing-line, and seeing the

"You must sit down on the wet grass whilst your attendant pulls them off, in order," &c.

To face page 34.

silk break about two feet above your hand;
then watching the broken end as it travels
quickly through each successive ring, till it
finally leaves the top of your rod, and follows
the fish to the bottom of the river.

XXIV.

Receiving a very elegant new rod from
London, and being told by one of the most
skilful of your brother anglers, that it is so
stiff,—and by another, that it is so pliant, that
it is not possible for any man to throw a
fly properly with it.

XXV.

Being obliged to listen to a long story
about the difficulties which one of your
friends had to encounter in landing a very
fine trout which has just been placed on the
table for dinner, when you have no story of
the same sort to tell in return.

D 2

XXVI.

Hooking a large trout, and then turning the handle of your reel the wrong way; thus producing an effect diametrically opposite to that of shortening your line, and making the fish more unmanageable than before.

XXVII.

Arriving just before sunset at a shallow, where the fish are rising beautifully, and finding that they are all about to be immediately driven away by five-and-twenty cows, which are preparing to walk very leisurely across the river in open files.

XXVIII.

Coming to an ugly ditch in your way across a water-meadow late in the day, when you are too tired to jump, and being obliged to walk half a mile in search of a place where you think you can step over it.

" Finding that they are all about to be immediately driven away by
five-and-twenty cows."

To-face page 36.

XXIX.

Flattering yourself that you had brought home the largest fish of the day, and then finding that two of your party have each of them caught a trout more than half a pound heavier than your's.

XXX.

Finding yourself reduced to the necessity of talking about the beautiful form and colour of some trout, which you have caught, being well aware that in the important particular of *weight,* they are much inferior to several of those taken on the same day by one of your companions.

XXXI.

Telling a long story after dinner, tending to show (with full particulars of time and place) how that, under very difficult circumstances, and notwithstanding very great skill on your part, your tackle had been that morning broken and carried away by a very large fish; and then having the identical fly, lost by you on that occasion, returned to you by one of your party, who found it in the mouth of a trout, caught by him, about an hour after your disaster, on the very spot so accurately described by you—the said very large fish being, after all, a very small one.

XXXII.

Arriving at a friend's house in the country, one very cold evening in March, and being told by his keeper that there are a great many large pike in the water, and that you are sure of having good sport on the following day; and then looking out of your bed-room window the next morning, and seeing two unhappy swans dancing an awkward sort of minuet on the ice, the surface of the lake having been completely frozen during the night.

R. P.

London,
March, 1833.

F. R. Lee, Esq., R.A.

MORE MISERIES.

(Continuation of Story from page 24.)

On a subsequent occasion our honest anglers repeated their visit to Mr. Jenkins, who, with the view of making himself more agreeable to his guests, had, in the meantime, agreed to pay an annual rent to the miller, for the exclusive right of fishing in some water belonging to the mill, which was said to contain the largest fish in the river.

Now, this miller had a son, who, whilst he followed his father's daily occupation of preparing matter for the *loaves,* sometimes thought of the *fishes* too; and he was better known in the neighbourhood for his great skill in fishing, than for any unusual acquaintance with the mysteries of grinding. He had frequently used much argument and entreaty to dissuade his father from letting the fishery; but the prudent old miller thought that £15 per annum, to be paid by Mr. Jenkins, would be more profitable to him, than any pleasure which his son might derive from catching many fine brace of trout during the season.

Such was the state of affairs in this part of the world, when Mr. Jackson and Mr. Thompson arrived early one morning, by special invitation, to make a first trial of their skill in the new water. The usual conversation about the state of the weather was quickly despatched at breakfast. The wind was, for once, pronounced to be in the right quarter. It was unanimously agreed that there could not well be a more favourable day for fishing, and that, therefore, the gentlemen ought to lose no time in going down to the river. Our old friend, Thompson, who, as we have already seen, was not always very successful with a fly, had lately, in order that he might have two strings to his bow*, been

---

* It was a long one, when he talked about fishing.

" He now sallied forth, not ' equal to both,' but ' armed for either field.' "

To face page 43.

learning another branch of the gentle art, called " Spinning a minnow;" and he now sallied forth, not " equal to both," but "armed for either field," and walked with a confident step to a celebrated spot below the mill. This new acquirement had been kept a profound secret from Jackson, who went out, as usual, fly-fishing, and proceeded to a part of the stream above the mill.

It was not to be expected that the young miller would work cheerfully at the mill that morning. He felt that, although he had been cruelly deprived of the fishery by his father, he surely had a right to *look* at the gentlemen if he pleased; he therefore put on his dusty hat and walked, in a surly mood, to the river side,—taking with him, as the companion of his sorrows, a ragged little boy, who had often witnessed his exploits with envy and admiration, and occasionally imitated his great example in a very humble manner by fishing for gudgeons in the canal.

The youth and the boy found Thompson
so busily engaged in arranging his new
spinning-tackle, that he did not perceive that
they had established themselves within a few
yards of him.   There he stood upon the bank,
deeply impressed with the value of some
excellent instructions which he had lately
received for his guidance, and fully sensible
of the vast superiority over Jackson which he
now possessed.   Having at last settled every
preliminary to his entire satisfaction, he was
just about to cast in his minnow for the first
time, when the miller attracted Thompson's
notice by that peculiar sort of short cough
which is a relief to suppressed insolence, and
acts as a safety-valve to prevent explosion.

Poor Thompson!   He did not feel quite
qualified for a performance of the kind
before a critic so well able to judge, and so
little disposed to admire; but he considered
that it would be *infra dig.* to appear discon-
certed by the young miller's presence,—so

he assumed a look of defiance, and manfully commenced operations.

After one or two bad throws, and sundry awkward attempts at improvement, a fine trout (*mirabile dictu!*) darted from under the bank and seized his minnow. "Who cares for the miller now?" thought Thompson; but, alas! the happy thought passed through his mind—

"Too like the lightning, which doth cease to be
Ere one can say—It lightens."

He unfortunately (vide Maxim IX.) held the fish a little too hard against the stream, and pulled him so very triumphantly, that the thrilling sensation of tugging pressure on the rod suddenly ceased, and the hookless end of the broken line flew into the air!!

At this awful crisis the young miller's cough became very troublesome, and the boy coolly called out to him—

*" I say, Jack!—I'll lay a penny that
wouldn't ha' happened if you had had hold
on 'im!!!"*

*   *   *   *

Long before Thompson had recovered
from the effects of this sad disaster, Jenkins
came up to him to announce that luncheon
was ready. Overwhelming our poor sufferer
with a torrent of well-meant condolence, he
said—

" Well, Thompson!

" What! no sport?

" That *is* unlucky!

" I am very anxious that *you* should catch
a good fish. *Jackson* has just caught a
brace of very fine ones!

" This is exactly the spot where I expected
that you would have the best sport!

" The miller tells me that the largest fish
lie there*, near that broken post under the

---

* There the fish did not *lie*, but the miller did. He
well knew that, since the letting of the fishery, his son

" I'll lay a penny that wouldn't ha' happened if you had hold on 'im !!"

To face page 46.

opposite bank. Pray cast your minnow close
to that, and you will be sure to run a fish
almost immediately."

Jenkins little knew what he was asking.
The aforesaid post was at a formidable distance,—it could only be reached by a most
skilful hand. Thompson felt by no means
disposed to attempt it, because, although
Jenkins appeared to think that it would be
an easy task for so finished an angler as
Thompson, he himself had no doubt that the
odious miller, who was still looking on, was
of a very different opinion. He therefore
thought that it would be wise to leave the
question undetermined, and not to give a
casting vote on the occasion.

And now Thompson, turning his back on
the river, walked home arm-in-arm with his
friend Mr. Jenkins, grieving much about the

---

had taken good care that the best of them should be gradually removed to Billingsgate by a more summary pro-
cess than that of rod and line.

fish which he had lost, and perhaps a little about those which Jackson had caught.

The brace of very fine trout, said to have been caught by Mr. Jackson, were exhibited by him in due form to Mr. Thompson and the ladies, just before luncheon. Whilst he was pointing out the beautiful condition of the fish, without at all underrating their weight, Miss Smith, who was staying on a visit with her sister, Mrs. Jenkins, pleasantly remarked that Mr. Jackson was very *lucky* to have caught two such fine fish whilst Mr. Thompson had not caught any. This led to an interesting conversation about the caprice of the fickle goddess, so often alluded to in the lamentations of an unsuccessful angler. Thompson took no part in the discussion, and he did not refer them to the miller or the little boy for any other explanation * of the

---

* Neither did Mr. Jackson think it necessary to explain to the ladies, or even to his friend Thompson, that the very fine fish, about which he had received so many compli-

Geo. Jones, Esq. R.A.

"He begged that they would allow him to eat his luncheon without
waiting for the rest of the party."

To face page 49.

cause of his failure; but he begged that they would allow him to eat his luncheon, without waiting for the rest of the party, as he was anxious to return as soon as possible to the river, where he expected to have great sport in the evening.

After luncheon, our unfortunate hero did not catch any fish, and he found that he could not throw his minnow within several yards of the far-famed post, even when he was not annoyed by spectators. He contrived, however, to get fast hold of another, at a much less distance from him; in consequence of which, he was obliged to abandon a second set of his best minnow tackle (price 2s. 6d.) to its fate in the middle of the river.

---

ments, had been taken by fixing his landing-net at the mouth of one of the narrow water-courses, up which they had worked their way in search of minnows;—a secret method of ensuring good sport, well known to some few very cunning anglers, whose motto is

" Unde habeas quærit Nemo, sed oportet habere."—Juv.

E

At the end of *his day's sport*, Thompson omitted to use the wise precaution of taking his rod to pieces*, before leaving the river side. On his way homewards, in the evening, he met the little boy, who slily asked him if he had had good sport *since*. This brought to his recollection the fact of his having to pass through the mill, in order to cross the river; and the prospect of his being asked a similar question by the miller was not agreeable. When he arrived at the mill, all was quiet; and he, therefore, flattered himself that the miller was comfortably enjoying his pipe at the ale-house.—Thompson was now so elated at the idea of passing through unobserved, that he quite forgot the exalted state of his rod, until

---

* I understand that Thompson has written a long letter, complaining of my not having given any maxim or hint on this important point. I beg leave here to apologise for the omission; and I have no hesitation in advising him, if he should ever put his rod together again, not to omit taking it to pieces as soon as he has done fishing.

"His ears were assailed by a loud repetition of the cruel cough."

To face page 51.

he was reminded of it by a sudden jerk which
broke off the top, leaving his third and last set
of tackle, with a brilliant artificial minnow,
sticking fast in a projecting rafter * above
his reach. Hastily shoving the broken joint
(Thompson never swears) into the butt of
his rod, he hoped that he should be able to
conceal all knowledge of this last misfortune.
He, however, felt very unwilling that the
shining little minnow should remain in its
present position, as a glaring proof of his
awkwardness; and it immediately occurred to
him, that a small ladder, which was close at
hand, was a thing exactly suited to the occasion; but at the very moment when he became convinced, by actual experiment, that it
was too short for his purpose, his ears were
assailed by a loud repetition of the cruel
cough, and his eyes were met by a killing
glance from those of the miller's son.

* Piscium et summâ genus hæsit ulmo.—Hor.

E 2

On the following day, Thompson returned, much out of spirits, to London. On that day, too, the young miller resumed his duties at the mill, less out of humour than before. Very shortly after this the old miller died, and the son then took the fishery into his own hands; and, however closely he may now resemble his late grandfather (who formerly lived on the River Dee), in caring for nobody, he never, whilst Thompson lives, will be able to say " Nobody cares for me."

"So ends my Tale :" for I fear that the reader must think that, like Thompson, he has now had quite enough of " THE MISE-RIES OF FISHING." I feel, however, assured that he will forgive me for relating this story, because, although his attention may be fatigued by the perusal of it, his eye will be gratified by the beauty of several new illustrations, which I owe to the kindness of my friends, the distinguished artists, whose names are printed under their welcome contributions to my little book.

R. P.

Whitehall,
March, 1839.

Sir Francis Chantrey, R.A.

MAXIMS AND HINTS

FOR A

CHESS PLAYER.

"*Lorsque je veux, sans y faire semblant, me livrer*
"*aux méditations d'une douce philosophie, je vais*
"*à la péche. Ma longue expérience me tient en*
"*garde contre les inconveniens d'une mauvaise pra-*
"*tique; et je jouis de mon succès, qu'aucun jaloux ne*
"*vient troubler. Ma péche finie, eh bien! je rentre*
"*dans le mouvement de la vie, je fais ma partie*
"*d'échecs; je triomphe, mon sang circule; je suis*
"*battu, mais je me releve.*"—TACTIQUE DES RE-
CREATIONS.

MAXIMS AND HINTS

FOR A

CHESS PLAYER.

I.

WIN as often as you can, but never make any display of insulting joy on the occasion. When you cannot win—lose (though you may not like it) with good temper.

II.

If your adversary, after you have won a game, wishes to prove that you have done so in consequence of some fault of his rather than by your own good play, you need not enter into much argument on the subject, whilst he is explaining to the by-standers the mode by which he might have won the game, *but did not.*

III.

Nor need you make yourself uneasy if your adversary should console himself by pointing out a mode by which you might have won the game in a shorter and more masterly manner. Listen patiently to his explanation —it cannot prove that your way was not good enough. *Tous les chemins sont bons qui mènent à la victoire.*

IV.

When you are playing with an opponent whom you feel sure that you can master, do not insult him by saying that you consider him a stronger player than yourself,—but that perhaps particular circumstances may prevent him from playing with his usual force to-day, &c. &c. Men usually play as well as they can: 'they are glad when they win, and sorry when they lose.

V.

Sometimes—when, alas! you have lost the game—an unmerciful conqueror will insist on " murdering Pizarro all over again," and glories in explaining how that your game was irretrievable after you had given a certain injudicious check with the queen,* (the consequence of which *he says* that he immediately foresaw,) and that then, by a succession of very good moves on his part, he won easily. You must bear all this as well as you can, although it is certainly not fair to "preach'ee and flog'ee too."

---

* *Infandum Regina jubes renovare dolorem.*

VI.

A good player seldom complains that another is slow. He is glad to have the opportunity thus afforded to him of attentively considering the state of the game. Do not, therefore, be impatient when it is your adversary's turn to move. Take as much time as you require (*and no more*) when it is your own turn.

VII.

If, whilst you are playing, your adversary will talk about the state of the game, it is very provoking, but you cannot help it, and the pieces will give you ample revenge, if you can avail yourself of their power.

VIII.

If the by-standers talk, it is still more annoying: they always claim the merit of having foreseen every good move which is made, and they sometimes express great sur-

prise at your not making a particular move ;
which, if you had made it, would probably
have led to your speedily losing the game—
before which time they would have walked
away to another table.

IX.

Almost every moderate player thinks himself fully qualified to criticise the move by
which a game has been lost.—Although, if
he had himself been in the loser's place, he
would, very probably, have been check-mated
twenty moves sooner than the opportunity occurred for committing the particular mistake,
which he thinks he should have avoided.

X.

Amongst good players, it is considered to
be as much an indispensable condition of the
game, that a piece once touched must be
moved, as that the queen is not allowed to
have the knight's, or a rook the bishop's
move.

XI.

Some persons, when they are playing with
a stranger who entreats to be allowed to take
back a move, let him do so the first time :
then, almost immediately afterwards, they put
their own queen *en prise;* and when the
mistake is politely pointed out to them, they
say that *they* never take back a move, but
that they are ready to begin another game.

XII.

Do not be alarmed about the state of your
adversary's health, when, after losing two
or three games, he complains of having a bad
head-ache, or of feeling very unwell. If he
should win the next game, you will probably
hear no more of this.

XIII.

Never (if you can avoid it) lose a game to
a person who rarely wins when he plays with
you. If you do so, you may afterwards find
that this one game has been talked of to all

his friends, although he may have forgotten to mention ninety-nine others which had a different result. Chess players have a very retentive memory with regard to the games which they win.

XIV.

If, therefore, any one should tell you that on a certain day last week he won a game from one of your friends, it may be as well to ask how many other games were played on the same day.

XV.

There is no better way of deciding on the comparative skill of two players than by the result of a number of games. Be satisfied with that result, and do not attempt to reason upon it.

XVI.

Remember the Italian proverb, " Never make a good move without first looking out for a better." Even if your adversary should

leave his queen *en prise*, do not snap hastily
at it. The queen is a good thing to win,
but the game is a better.

XVII.

Between even, and tolerably good, players
a mere trifle frequently decides the event of
a game; but when you have gained a small
advantage, you must be satisfied with it for
the time. Do not, by attempting too much,
lose that which you have gained. Your object
should be to win the game, and the dullest
way of winning is better for you than the
most brilliant of losing.

XVIII.

If your knowledge of "the books" enables
you to see that a person, with whom you are
playing for the first time, opens his game
badly, do not suppose, as a matter of course,
that you are going to check-mate him in ten
or twelve moves. Many moves called *very*

bad are only such if well opposed; and you can derive but little advantage from them unless you are well acquainted with the system of crowding your adversary,—one of the most difficult parts of the game.

XIX.

Some players have by study acquired mechanically the art of opening their game in a style much above their real force; but when they have exhausted their store of *book-knowledge*, they soon fall all to pieces, and become an easy prey to those who have genuine talent for the game. Others do not know how to open their game on scientific principles, and yet, if they can stagger through the beginning without decided loss, fight most nobly when there are but few pieces and pawns left on the board. All these varieties of play must be carefully studied by those who wish to win. It is only talent for the game, combined with much study and

F

great practice, which can make a truly good player.

XX.

Although no degree of instruction derived from " books" will make a good player, without much practice with all sorts of opponents, yet, on the other hand, when you hear a person, who has had great practice, boast of never having looked into a chess-book, you may be sure either that he is a bad player, or that he is not nearly so good a player as he might become by attentively studying the laborious works which have been published on almost every conceivable opening, by such players as Ercole del Rio, Ponziani, Philidor, Sarratt, and Lewis.

XXI.

Between fine players, small odds (viz. pawn, with one, or with two moves) are of great consequence.   Between inferior players they are of none. The value of these odds consists chiefly in position; and in every long game between weak players, such an advantage is gained and lost several times, without either party being aware of it.

XXII.

Almost all good players (*and some others*) have a much higher opinion of their own strength than it really deserves. One person feels sure that he is a better player than some particular opponent, although he cannot but confess that, for some unaccountable reason, or other, he does not always win a majority of games from him. Another attributes his failure solely to want of attention to details which he considers hardly to involve any real genius for the game; and he is obliged to content himself with boasting of having certainly, at one time, had much the best of a game, which he afterwards lost, *only by a mistake*. A third thinks that he

must be a good player, because he has dis-
covered almost all the many difficult check-
mates which have been published as pro-
blems.   He may be able to do this, and yet
be unable to play a whole game well, it being
much more easy to find out, at your leisure,
the way to do that which you are told before-
hand is practicable, than to decide, in actual
play, whether, or not, it is prudent to make
the attempt.

XXIII.

A theoretical amateur, with much real
genius for the game, is often beaten by a
fourth-rate player at a chess club, who has
become from constant practice thoroughly
acquainted with all the technicalities of it,
and quietly builds up a wall for the other
to run his head against.   The loser in this
case may *perhaps* eventually become the
better player of the two; but he is not so at
present.

XXIV.

A person sometimes tells you that he played the other day, for the first time, with Mr. Such-a-one, (a very celebrated player,) who won the game, with great difficulty, after a very hard fight. Your friend probably deceives himself greatly in supposing this to be the case. A player who has a reputation to lose, always plays very cautiously against a person whose strength he does not yet know: he runs no risks, and does not attempt to do more than win the game, which is all that he undertook to do.

XXV.

When you receive the odds of a piece from a better player than yourself, remember he sees everything which you see, and probably much more. Be very careful how you attack him. You must act in the early part of the game entirely on the defensive, or probably you will not live long enough to enjoy the advantage which has been given you. Even though you may still have the advantage of a piece more, when the game is far advanced, you must not feel too sure of victory. Take all his pawns quietly, *if you can*, and see your way clearly before you attempt to check-mate him. You will thus perhaps be longer about it, but winning is very agreeable work.

XXVI.

Many persons advise you, when you re-ceive the odds of a rook, *always* to make exchanges as often as you can, in order to maintain the numerical superiority with which you began. This is very cunning; but you will probably find that *" Master is York-shire too,"* and that he will not allow you to make exchanges early in the game, except under circumstances which lead you into a ruinous inferiority of position.

XXVII.

You will never improve by playing only with players of your own strength. In order to play well, you must toil through the humiliating task of being frequently beaten by those who can give you odds. These odds, when you have fairly mastered them, may be gradually diminished as your strength increases. Do not, however, deceive yourself by imagining, that if you cannot win from one of the *great players* when he gives you the odds of a rook, you would stand a better chance with the odds of a knight. This is a very common error. It is true that, when a knight is given, the attack made upon you is not so sudden and so violent, as it usually is when you receive a rook—but your ultimate defeat is much more certain. If, in the one case, you are quickly killed, in the other you will die in lingering torments.

XXVIII.

When you hear of a man from the country, who has beaten every body whom he has ever played with, do not suppose, as a matter of course, that he is a truly good player. He may be only a " Triton of the Minnows." All his fame depends upon the skill of the parties with whom he has hitherto contended ; and provincial Philidors seldom prove to be very good players, when their strength is fairly measured at the London Chess Club, particularly such of them as come there with the reputation of having never been beaten.

XXIX.

An elderly gentleman, lately returned from India, is apt to suppose that his skill has been much impaired by the change of climate, or some other cause, when he finds, to his great surprise, that his style of play does not produce such an alarming effect in the Chess

Clubs of London or Paris, as it used to do at Rumbarabad.

XXX.

When you can decidedly win, at the odds of a rook given by a first-rate player, you will rank among the chosen few. It would be very difficult to name twenty-five persons in London to whom Mr. Lewis could not fairly give these odds, although there are many hundreds who would be much offended at its being supposed to be possible that any one could give them a knight.

XXXI.

A first-rate player, who is to give large odds to a stranger, derives great advantage from seeing him first play a game, or two, with other persons. His style of play is thus shown, and the class of risks which may be ventured on is nicely calculated. That which, before, might have been difficult, thus becomes comparatively easy.

XXXII.

There is as much difference between playing a game well, by correspondence, and
playing one well over the board, as there is
between writing a good essay, and making a
good speech.

XXXIII.

No advantages of person and voice will
enable a man to become a good orator if he
does not understand the grammatical con-
struction of the language in which he speaks:
nor will the highest degree of ingenuity make
any man a good chess player, unless his pre-
parations for the exercise of that ingenuity
are made upon the soundest principles of the
game.

XXXIV.

Every game perfectly played throughout
on both sides would be by its nature drawn.
Since, then, in matches between the most celebrated players and clubs of the day some of
the games have been won and lost, it seems

to follow that there *might* be better players
than have been hitherto known to exist.

XXXV.

Most of the persons who occasionally " play
at Chess" know little more than the moves
and a few of the general rules of the game.
Of those who have had more practice, some
have acquired a partial insight into the end-
less variety of the combinations which may
be formed, and their beautiful intricacy :—a
few play moderately well ; but, however small
the number of good players may be, it would
be difficult to find any one who, after having
played a few hundred games, would not
think it an imputation on his good sense to
be considered a very bad player ;—and this is
the universal feeling, although it is well
known that men of the highest attainments
have studied Chess without great success ;
and that the most celebrated players have not
always been men of distinguished talents.

XXXVI.

He who after much practice with fine players remains for a long time without taking his station amongst them, will find at last that there is a point which he cannot pass. He is obliged to confess his incurable inferiority to players of the higher order, and he must be content with easy victories over a large majority of those whom he meets with in society.

CONCLUSION.

Chess holds forth to the philosopher relaxation from his severer studies,—to the disappointed man, relief from unavailing regret, —and to the rich and idle, an inexhaustible source of amusement and occupation. It has, however, been frequently urged as an objection to the study of the game, that no man can pursue it, with a fair prospect of becoming a good player, without devoting to it much time and attention which might be more beneficially employed.

Although it may perhaps be true in the abstract, that even a high degree of skill is not *per se* worth the time and trouble which it must have cost, it should be remembered that on this " mimic stage " of life much besides chess may be seen and studied with advantage. The real character of a man's mind may, almost always, be known by his behaviour under the varying circumstances

of this most interesting game. The triumph
of the winner, and the vexation of the loser,
are often coarsely displayed amongst inferior
players; and, although good players very
rarely give way to this degrading weakness,
still, the good breeding of some of them,
towards the end of a difficult match, is not
always quite perfect.

The temper of the student cannot fail to
derive very material benefit from the severe
discipline to which it will be subjected.
When he begins to play well he will find that
he has learnt to submit patiently to contradiction; and that he has become convinced of
the necessity of abandoning his most fa-
vourite schemes, whenever he sees that from
a change of circumstances they can be no
longer pursued with safety.—He will have
felt the full value of using caution and circum-
spection, when called upon to exercise his
judgment in cases of complicated difficulty,
and he will have acquired the faculty of

fixing his undivided attention on the business in which he is engaged.

If such qualities of the mind are called forth and strengthened in the pursuit of a harmless and delightful recreation, the time cannot have been wholly wasted, although the professed object of study may have been only the art of giving CHECK-MATE.

R. P.

Whitehall, March, 1839.

London: Printed by WILLIAM CLOWES and Sons, Stamford Street.

CPSIA information can be obtained at www.ICGtesting.com
Printed in the USA
BVOW05s1905200616

452771BV00021B/242/P